PUGS
IN COSTUMES

3 5 7 9 10 8 6 4

Published in 2014 by Virgin Books, an imprint of Ebury Publishing

A Random House Group Company

The Random House Group Limited Reg. No. 954009

Addresses for companies within the Random House Group can be found at
www.randomhouse.co.uk

A CIP catalogue record for this book is available from the British Library

The Random House Group Limited supports The Forest Stewardship Council® (FSC®), the leading international forest–certification organisation. Our books carrying the FSC label are printed on FSC®–certified paper. FSC is the only forest–certification scheme supported by the leading environmental organisations, including Greenpeace. Our paper procurement policy can be found at www.randomhouse.co.uk/environment

To buy books by your favourite authors and register for offers visit
www.randomhouse.co.uk

Design by ClarkevanMeurs Design Ltd

Printed and bound in Italy by Printer Trento

ISBN 9780753556054

PUGS
IN COSTUMES

WOOD

Pugs of stage and screen

MARILYN PUG ROE

WIZARD OF PUG

PUGIANA JONES

CAPTAIN PUG

ELVIS PUGSLEY

MEMOIRS OF A GEISHA PUG

EDWARD SCISSORPUG

PUGERACE

GONE WITH THE WIND

SCARLETT O'PUGRA

PUG STORY

SNOW WHITE PUG

GANDALF THE GREY PUG

PUGS OF MIDDLE EARTH

MILEY WRECKING BALL PUG

BOB PUGLEY

TEENAGE MUTANT NINJA **PUG**

THE LION PUG

I DREAM OF JEANNIE PUG

THE INCREDIBLE PUG

PUG, I AM

CHEWPUGCA AND PUG VADER

CHRISTINA PUG-ILERA

I WANT YOU

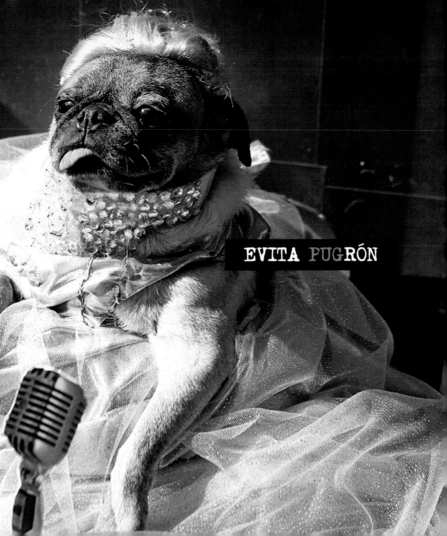

EVITA PUGRÓN

THRILLER PUGS

SWEET PUG O' MINE

I LOVE LUCY PUG

ROBIN PUG

PLAYPUG

THE VILLAGE PUGS

THE PUG OF WALL STREET

THE PUG OF THE BASKERVILLES

JACKIE O PUG

ELECT A PUG

PRESIDENT PUG

ELECT A PUG

VEEN

Trick or treat pugs

PUGKIN

MOO PUG

AMELIA EAR**PUG**

PUGRITO

CHICKEN KUNG PUG

CINCO DE PUGO

COUNT PUGULA

SPIDER PUG

PUGLICE

SPORTS PUG

CLEOPUGRA

ANNA PUGLOVA

DINOPUG

BAT PUG

PIERROT PUG

PUGSTOCK

BEELZIPUG

LADYPUG

PUG**CASSO**

AMERICAN PUGBALL

PUGGERFLY

SCUBA PUG

SAILOR PUG

FROG PUG

BAD PUG!

GRAND NATIONAL PUG

PAWS

GORDON PUGSAY

MARIE-PUGTOINETTE

ELEPUG

POPPY PUGS

ROYAL PUG

NIKKI PUGAJ

CALIFORNIA PUG

G.I. PUG

WOOLLY MAMMOTH PUG

BUSH PUG

LITTLE RED RIDING PUG

CAPTAIN PUGWASH

LOBSTER PUG

FRIDGE MAGNET PUG

AMERICAN EAGLE PUG

THE GOOD, THE BAD AND THE PUGLY

SEÑOR PUG

MINNIE PUG

PEA**PUG**

FIREMAN PUG

MARVIN THE MARTIAN PUG

SQUIRREL PUG

ANGEL PUG

PEASANT PUG

ZEBRA PUG

TINKERPUG

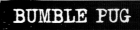
BUMBLE PUG

BAILEY

PUG IN A PUG

UTURE

Best-dressed pugs in town

WEDDING PUGS

LOVE PUG

PIN-UP PUG

GLAMOUR PUG

PINK PUG

VIVIENNE WESTPUG

FAIRY PUG

BJORK PUG

PUGBACK MOUNTAIN

ST PUGRICK'S DAY

EASTER PUG

MAMA PUG

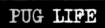

JAPUGNESE

PUG NO. 5

FLAPPER PUG

Picture Credits

Pg 6. Marilyn Pugroe – Kiwi – Janet Barrington
Pg 7. Superpug - Ben Koker / Oregon Humane Society
Pg 8 –9. Wizard of Pug – Ivan and Roxy – Reuters / Mike Blake / Corbis
Pg 10. Pugiana Jones – Lightning– Paul Epps
Pg 11. Captain Pug – Russell Scheid
Pg 12. Elvis Pugsley – Jasper– Mandel Ngan/AFP/ Getty Images
Pg 13. Memoirs of a Geisha Pug – Mouchi and Olive – Richard Vogel/ AP/ PA
Pg 14. Edward ScissorPug – Sipa Press/ Rex Features
Pg 15. Pugerace – Kiwi – Janet Barrington
Pg 16. Scarlett O Pugra – Gracie – Timothy Clary/ AFP/Getty Images
Pg 17. Mr Pugagi - Blue - Phillip Lauer www.pupstarsonoma.com
Pg 18. Pug Story – Joe Blusys
Pg 19. Snow White Pug – Rick Harris / pugalug.com
Pg 20. Gandalf the Grey Pug – Blue – Phillip Lauer/ **www.pupstarsonoma.com**
Pg 21. Pugs of Middle Earth – Bono and Blue – Phillip Lauer/ www.pupstarsonoma.com
Pg 22. Miley Wrecking Ball – Tottie – McKenna
Pg 23. Bubble Pug – Roxy – Sue / Ruth Wedge
Pg 24. Teenage Mutant Ninja Pug – Ben Koker / Oregon Humane Society
Pg 25. PugZilla – Ben Koker/Oregon Humane Society
Pg 26. The Lion Pug – Douglas Smith / Getty Images
Pg 27. K–9 Pug – Ben Koker/ Oregon Humane Society
Pg 28. I Dream of Jeannie Pug – Kiwi / Janet Barrington
Pg 29. The Incredible Pug – Ben Koker/ Oregon Humane Society
Pg 30. Pug AM – Buster McKibben – Julia Shevchenko
Pg 31. ChewPugca and Pug Vader – Ben Koker / Oregon Humane Society
Pg 32. Christina Pugilera – Kiwi – Janet Barrington
Pg 33. Evita Pugron – Mario Hagopian / Splash News / Corbis
Pg 34 – 35. Thriller Pugs – Rudy and Parker / Mario Tama/Getty Images
Pg 36. Sweet Pug O Mine – Blue – Phillip Lauer / www.pupstarsonoma.com
Pg 37. I Love Lucy Pug – Kiwi – Janet Barrington
Pg 38. Robin Pug – Bono – Phillip Lauer / www.pupstarsonoma.com
Pg 39. PlayPug – Maya – Erica Sommers
Pg 40–41. Village Pugs – Erica Sommers
Pg 42. The Pug of Wall Street – Pukster – Terry Alcorn / Getty Images
Pg 43. The Pug of the Baskervilles – Rainer Elstermann / Getty Images
Pg 44. Jackie O Pug – Kiwi – Janet Barrington
Pg 45. President Pug – Ben Koker – Oregon Humane Society

Pg 48. Pugkin – Collette – Mario Tama / Getty Images
Pg 49. Moo Pug – Squishy – ZUMA Press / Alamy
Pg 50. Amelia Earpug – Jessica Furtado http:// allyouneedispug.com
Pg 51. Percy Pug – Hercules – Amy Conn/ AP /PA
Pg 52. Pugrito – Joe Blusys
Pg 53. Chicken Kung Pug – Ms Ping – Mario Tama/ Getty Images
Pg 54. Cinco de Pugo – Kiwi – Janet Barrington
Pg 55. Count Pugula – Rick Harris / Pugalug.com
Pg 56. Spider Pug – Odin – Nick Savage / Alamy
Pg 57. Puglice – Soliel – AP/ PA
Pg 58. Sports Pug – Rick Harris / Pugalug.com
Pg 59. Cleopugra – Kiwi – Janet Barrington
Pg 60. Anna Puglova – Minnie –Rick Madonik / AP / PA
Pg 61. DinoPug Joe Blusys
Pg 62. Bat Pug – Boris – Paul Brown / Alamy
Pg 63. Pierrot Pug – FLPA / Alamy
Pg 64. Pugstock – Joe Blusys
Pg 65. Beelzipug – Archie – Dee McCracken
Pg 66. LadyPug – Lilly – Linda Lombardi
Pg 67. Pugcasso – Elmer – Sue
Pg 68. America Pugball – Boise Pug Meetup Group
Pg 69. Puggerfly – Little Buddha – Jill Hamilton – Krawczyk
Pg 70. Scuba Pug – Elmer – Sue / Ruth Wedge
Pg 71. Sailor – Bella – Erica Sommers
Pg 72. Frog Pug – Elliot – Allison Snider – Steve Kohls A /PA
Pg 73. Bad Pug – Odie – Enid Alvarez/NY Daily News Archive via Getty Images
Pg 74. Grand National Pug –Franziska Kraufmann / PA
Pg 75. Pugdini – Kiwi – Janet Barrington
Pg 76. Pugwatch – Blue, Roxy, Bono – Phillip Lauer www.pupstarsonoma.com
Pg 77. Paws – Lilly – Linda Lombardi
Pg 78. Gordon Pugsay – Riley Steven –Pugs and Kisses / www.pugsandkisses.com
Pg 79. Marie Pugtoinette – Sara Bogush
Pg 80. Elepug – Jessica Furtado www.allyouneedispug.com
Pg 81. Poppy Pugs – Mochi and Olive / Lisa Woodruff – Richard Vogel AP / PA
Pg 82. Royal Pug – Roxy – Phillip Lauer www.pupstarsonoma.com
Pg 83. Nikki Pugaj – Getty Images
Pg 84. California Pug – Roxy – Sue / Ruth Wedge
Pg 85. G.I. Pug – Pocky – Robyn Beck/AFP/Getty Images
Pg 86. Woolly Mammoth Pug – Rex Features
Pg 87. Bush Pug – Chia Pet Honeybear – John Chapple / Rex Features
Pg 88. Little Red Riding Hood – Richard Jones / Sinopix / Rex Features
Pg 89. Captain Pugwash – Tricky Fox – Paul Brown / Rex Features

Pg 90. Lobster Pug – Paul Brown / Rex Features
Pg 91. Fridge Magnet Pug – Harley John Chapple / Rex Features
Pg 92. American Eagle Pug – Izzy– Ben Koker / Oregon Humane Society
Pg 93. Cheer Pug – Elena Elisseeva / Alamy
Pg 94. The Good The Bad and The Pugly – Blue – Phillip Lauer www.pupstarsonoma.com
Pg 95. Senor Pug – Einstein – Paul Brown / Alamy
Pg 96. Minnie Pug – Jessica Furtado www.allyouneedispug.com
Pg 97. PeaPug – Maya – Erica Sommers
Pg 98. Fireman Pug – Phillippe Diederich / Getty Images
Pg 99. Marvin the Martian Pug – Kiwi – Janet Barrington
Pg 100. Squirrel Pug – Rick Harris / Pugalug.com
Pg 101. Angel Pug – Rick Harris / Puglalug.com
Pg 102. Peasant Pug – Sara Bogush
Pg 103. Zebra Pug – Jessica Furtado www.allyouneedispug.com
Pg 104. Rapugzel – Sara Bogush
Pg 105. TinkerPug – Bella – Erica Sommers
Pg 106. Bumble Pug – istock
Pg 107. Pug in a Pug – Bailey – Tina Moreau

PUG COUTURE

Pg 110. Wedding Pugs – Reuters / Rick Wilking / Corbis
Pg 111. Love Pug – Bailey – Tina Moreau
Pg 112. Pin-Up Pug – Chris Stein / Getty Images
Pg 113. Glamour Pug – Mamma Biscuit – www.mammabiscuit.com
Pg 114. Pink Pug – Clara Francis – Pugs and Kisses www.pugandkisses.com
Pg 115. Vivienne WestPug Mamma Biscuit – www.mammabiscuit.com
Pg 116. Fairy Pug – Clara Francis – Pugs and Kisses www.pugandkisses.com
Pg 117. Bjork Pug – Mamma Biscuit – www.mammabiscuit.com
Pg 118 – 119. Pugback Mountain – Roxy, Blue and Bono – Phillip Lauer www.pupstarsonoma.com
Pg 120. St Patrick's Day – Bandit – Gerald Brazell
Pg 121. Easter Pug – Clara Francis – Pugs and Kisses www.pugandkisses.com
Pg 122. Mama Pug – Jenny – Krystal Foster
Pg 123. Pug Life – Mamma Biscuit – www.mammabiscuit.com
Pg 124. Puganese – Penny – Robert Nickelsberg/ Getty Images
Pg125. Pug No. 5 – Mamma Biscuit – www.mammabiscuit.com
Pg 126. Flapper Pug – Gretta Rose – Pugs and Kisses www.pugandkisses.com
Pg127. Bah HumPug – Elmer and Roxy – Sue / Ruth Wedge